"I saw your glory and it dazzled me."
— St. Augustine

Date _____   **Speaker** _____

Topic _____

Scripture References
_____
_____

My Notes:

What "Speaks" To Me:

What I Will Implement This Week:

For Further Study:

Date _____   **Speaker** _____

Topic _____

Scripture References

_____
_____

My Notes:	What "Speaks" To Me:

For Further Study:

What I Will Implement This Week:

Date _____   **Speaker** _____

Topic _____

Scripture References

_____
_____

My Notes:

What "Speaks" To Me:

What I Will Implement This Week:

For Further Study:

Date _____   **Speaker** _____

Topic _____

Scripture References

_____
_____

My Notes:

What "Speaks" To Me:

What I Will Implement This Week:

For Further Study:

Date _____ **Speaker** _____

Topic _____

Scripture References
_____
_____

My Notes:

What "Speaks" To Me:

For Further Study:

What I Will Implement This Week:

Date _____   **Speaker** _____

Topic _____

Scripture References

My Notes:

What "Speaks" To Me:

What I Will Implement This Week:

For Further Study:

Date _____ **Speaker** _____

Topic _____

Scripture References
_____
_____

My Notes:

What "Speaks" To Me:

What I Will Implement This Week:

For Further Study:

Date _____ **Speaker** _____

Topic _____

Scripture References

_____
_____

My Notes:

What "Speaks" To Me:

What I Will Implement This Week:

For Further Study:

Date _____   **Speaker** _____

Topic _____

Scripture References
_____
_____

My Notes:

What "Speaks" To Me:

What I Will Implement This Week:

For Further Study:

Date _____   **Speaker** _____

Topic _____

Scripture References

_____

_____

My Notes:

What "Speaks" To Me:

What I Will Implement This Week:

For Further Study:

Date

Speaker

Topic

Scripture References

My Notes:

What "Speaks" To Me:

What I Will Implement This Week:

For Further Study:

Date _____   **Speaker** _____

Topic _____

Scripture References

_____
_____

My Notes:	What "Speaks" To Me:

	What I Will Implement This Week:
For Further Study:	

Date _____   **Speaker** _____

Topic _____

Scripture References

_____
_____

My Notes:

What "Speaks" To Me:

What I Will Implement This Week:

For Further Study:

Date _____   **Speaker** _____

Topic _____

Scripture References

_____
_____

My Notes:	What "Speaks" To Me:

For Further Study:	What I Will Implement This Week:

Date _____   **Speaker** _____

Topic _____

Scripture References

_____
_____

My Notes:	What "Speaks" To Me:

For Further Study:	What I Will Implement This Week:

Date _____   **Speaker** _____

Topic _____

Scripture References
_____
_____

My Notes:

What "Speaks" To Me:

What I Will Implement This Week:

For Further Study:

Date _____   **Speaker** _____

Topic _____

Scripture References

_____
_____

My Notes:

What "Speaks" To Me:

What I Will Implement This Week:

For Further Study:

Date _____   **Speaker** _____

Topic _____

Scripture References

_____
_____

My Notes:	What "Speaks" To Me:

For Further Study:	What I Will Implement This Week:

Date _____   **Speaker** _____

Topic _____

Scripture References
_____
_____

My Notes:

What "Speaks" To Me:

What I Will Implement This Week:

For Further Study:

Date _____ **Speaker** _____

Topic _____

Scripture References
_____
_____

My Notes:

What "Speaks" To Me:

What I Will Implement This Week:

For Further Study:

Date _____   **Speaker** _____

Topic _____

Scripture References

_____
_____

My Notes:

What "Speaks" To Me:

What I Will Implement This Week:

For Further Study:

Date _____ **Speaker** _____

Topic _____

Scripture References
_____
_____

My Notes:

For Further Study:

What "Speaks" To Me:

What I Will Implement This Week:

Date _____   **Speaker** _____

Topic _____

Scripture References

_____
_____

My Notes:	What "Speaks" To Me:

For Further Study:	What I Will Implement This Week:

Date _____   **Speaker** _____

Topic _____

Scripture References
_____
_____

My Notes:	What "Speaks" To Me:

For Further Study:

What I Will Implement This Week:

Date _____   **Speaker** _____

Topic _____

Scripture References
_____
_____

My Notes:

What "Speaks" To Me:

What I Will Implement This Week:

For Further Study:

Date _____   **Speaker** _____

Topic _____

Scripture References

_____

My Notes:

What "Speaks" To Me:

What I Will Implement This Week:

For Further Study:

Date _____   **Speaker** _____

Topic _____

Scripture References
_____
_____

My Notes:	What "Speaks" To Me:

For Further Study:	What I Will Implement This Week:

Date _____ **Speaker** _____

Topic _____

Scripture References
_____
_____

| My Notes: | What "Speaks" To Me: |

| For Further Study: | What I Will Implement This Week: |

Date _____   **Speaker** _____

Topic _____

Scripture References
_____
_____

My Notes:

What "Speaks" To Me:

What I Will Implement This Week:

For Further Study:

Date _____   **Speaker** _____

Topic _____

Scripture References

_____
_____

My Notes:

What "Speaks" To Me:

What I Will Implement This Week:

For Further Study:

Date _____   **Speaker** _____

Topic _____

Scripture References

_____
_____

My Notes:	What "Speaks" To Me:

For Further Study:

What I Will Implement This Week:

Date _____   **Speaker** _____

Topic _____

Scripture References

_____
_____

My Notes:	What "Speaks" To Me:

For Further Study:	What I Will Implement This Week:

Date _____   **Speaker** _____

Topic _____

Scripture References
_____
_____

My Notes:	What "Speaks" To Me:

What I Will Implement This Week:

For Further Study:

Date _____ **Speaker** _____

Topic _____

Scripture References

My Notes:

What "Speaks" To Me:

What I Will Implement This Week:

For Further Study:

Date _____   **Speaker** _____

Topic _____

Scripture References
_____
_____

My Notes:

What "Speaks" To Me:

What I Will Implement This Week:

For Further Study:

Date _____   **Speaker** _____

Topic _____

Scripture References

_____

_____

My Notes:

What "Speaks" To Me:

What I Will Implement This Week:

For Further Study:

Date _____ **Speaker** _____

Topic _____

Scripture References

_____

_____

My Notes:

What "Speaks" To Me:

What I Will Implement This Week:

For Further Study:

Date _____   **Speaker** _____

Topic _____

Scripture References

_____
_____

My Notes:

What "Speaks" To Me:

What I Will Implement This Week:

For Further Study:

Date _____   **Speaker** _____

Topic _____

Scripture References
_____
_____

My Notes:

What "Speaks" To Me:

What I Will Implement This Week:

For Further Study:

Date _____ **Speaker** _____

Topic _____

Scripture References
_____
_____

My Notes:

What "Speaks" To Me:

What I Will Implement This Week:

For Further Study:

Date _____ **Speaker** _____

Topic _____

Scripture References
_____
_____

My Notes:

What "Speaks" To Me:

What I Will Implement This Week:

For Further Study:

Date _____   **Speaker** _____

Topic _____

Scripture References

_____

My Notes:

What "Speaks" To Me:

What I Will Implement This Week:

For Further Study:

Date _____   **Speaker** _____

Topic _____

Scripture References
_____
_____

My Notes:

What "Speaks" To Me:

What I Will Implement This Week:

For Further Study:

Date _____   **Speaker** _____

Topic _____

Scripture References
_____
_____

My Notes:

What "Speaks" To Me:

What I Will Implement This Week:

For Further Study:

Date _____   **Speaker** _____

Topic _____

Scripture References

My Notes:

What "Speaks" To Me:

What I Will Implement This Week:

For Further Study:

Date _____ **Speaker** _____

Topic _____

Scripture References

_____

_____

My Notes:	What "Speaks" To Me:

For Further Study:

What I Will Implement This Week:

Date _____   **Speaker** _____

Topic _____

Scripture References
_____
_____

My Notes:

What "Speaks" To Me:

What I Will Implement This Week:

For Further Study:

Date _____   **Speaker** _____

Topic _____

Scripture References
_____
_____

My Notes:

What "Speaks" To Me:

What I Will Implement This Week:

For Further Study:

Date _____   **Speaker** _____

Topic _____

Scripture References

_____

_____

My Notes:	What "Speaks" To Me:

	What I Will Implement This Week:
For Further Study:	

Date _____   **Speaker** _____

Topic _____

Scripture References

_____

_____

My Notes:

What "Speaks" To Me:

What I Will Implement This Week:

For Further Study:

Date _____   **Speaker** _____

Topic _____

Scripture References

_____

_____

My Notes:	What "Speaks" To Me:

For Further Study:

What I Will Implement This Week:

Date

Speaker

Topic

Scripture References

My Notes:

What "Speaks" To Me:

What I Will Implement This Week:

For Further Study:

Made in the USA
Columbia, SC
18 November 2019